S A M S A R A

First Printing, 2020

Lulu Press Inc.
3101 Hillsborough Street,
Raleigh, NC 27606

www.lulu.com

Printed in the United States of America

about the author

Brenden Mariage was born on Feb. 16, 1996, in Kalamazoo, Michigan. His journey throughout life has been to share his experiences through writing and self-expression. His introductory poetry collection, *The Definition of Love;*, was released in March of 2016. Since the release, he has experienced monumental changes that have molded him into the person he is today. It is his belief that true progression is found through overcoming periods of time that create discomfort in the human condition.

If there is only one takeaway from these pages, let it be this:

Love more.

Contact Brenden through the following avenues:
email: brendenmariagepr@gmail.com
Instagram: brendenmariage

Dedication

-

To my mother, Mary, for instilling love, kindness and compassion into my life.

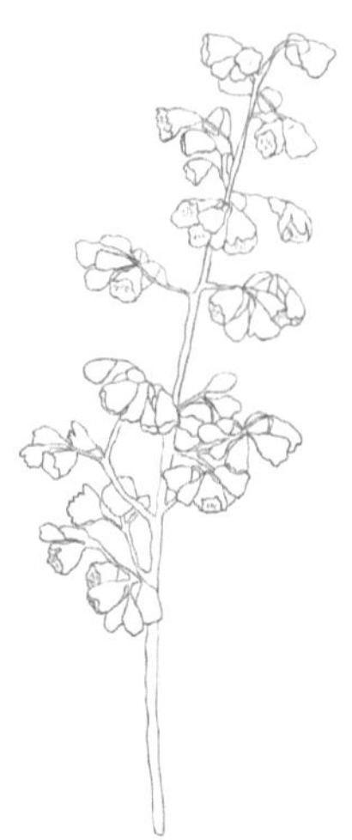

SAMSARA

from my experience
happiness is found in the aftermath
of sorrow

after

an acceptance of the things
we cannot control

your touch after a time
feels like warm honey running down my throat
through the ridges
the slowness is loving and careful
my mind lights up like a lamp post during a storm -
for a moment i can see the edges of you

if you are truly lasting
then the storm shall pass

it should be known that the present is
the only place where love and compassion can
thrive in the midst of instantaneous interactions

where we find our breaths and our heartbeat
is the place where we must reside in order
to understand what the world is showing us

there are moments in this world
where we find ourselves feeling lost
or not found
which leads to seeking answers
from a place
that is not ours
unknowing that the only place to
find answers
is within us

it may be time that
we redefine vulnerability
to fit a mold that doesn't
accompany weakness

no longer should it flow
alongside shame or fear
but with the waves of
compassionate love

your eyes mimic the warmth of a café miel
with cinnamon sprinkled across your
honey kissed lips

i hope you know that
your faults are nothing more
than the tension in your chest

you and i felt like a bonfire
in the woods on a cold night
that slowly - but inevitably
would die from our own devices

humans are like trees
in the sense that everything
of value and the things that keep us alive
grow beneath the surface and run deep
in order to help our consciousness flourish
like the leaves on the tree or the roots in
the ground
the outward beauty could not pose
if the lungs forgot to breathe

could we love one another
knowing what we know now

knowing our love was made
in the presence of ignorance

i’m aware of the nights allure
i have resided there for longer
than most
only to find peace in the moment
that the sun finds itself flooding into
my presence

too often i'm alone in a crowded room
a singular in the multiples
a drop in the mist
lost amongst the extroverts
a pawn unmoving in the room of life
dimensions flowing through veins
lost on the sea of wood floors
feeling the longing to be utterly alone
yet wanted

i know more women
who have been raped
than i know men
who admit that there
is a societal problem.

transparency is a virtue
the soul doesn't thrive when the air is cloudier
than the smog amongst the skies

to be free in one's heart compares
to the euphoria of living a life of wonders
to roam the heart and soul is to live a life
worth living.

naturally we find it hard to understand that
our flaws are the cause of an issue
to accept and understand that is to
be human

muddy faces don’t tell fallacies
they tell their truth, which just
happens to be a fallacy

i hear your voice in colors
and feel your touch in songs
i see your lips in my coffee cups
and i love you for the things you will never see

it's okay to feel things
even if they hurt sometimes
to feel things means to feel alive
or at least somewhat alive
even if you don't want to be
alive
that is, feeling this way isn't wrong
but life is precious and has meaning,
even though you don't see it right now
it's not that you live each day for yourself
but, to live this experience - this glimpse of history
the beauty of life
is unmatched
and i'd love to see you stay here
with us
even though sometimes you don't want to
sometimes i don't want to
but i know that staying here is my best bet
in the world that has flaws, we can make it better
i love
you.

when the light comes in the morning
the darkness finds its home over the hills
where the demons wait for the dying of the light

the days come
then the days go

until the break of the horizon finds the creases in the window curtains
where the dust settled long before the fault began to form.

she said it feels like
a hollowed hole in the tree of life
in the aftermath
the hole burns continuously
without hesitation for the tree

there is no healing
only living with the pain
with the memories of that day
forever

dim diner lights make for easy conversations
in the night time where the thoughts linger through passages
through a multitude of decisions and thoughts
until one car is left in the lot
with no one to take it home.

truth is the core to reality
in the truth, there is light and clarity
in the depths of lies, there is the absence of hope.

the ways in which we maneuver the depths
is a journey we venture alone -
afraid and uncertain.

is it true or is it my mind
is it love or is it lust
the thoughts that consume us will inevitably be our downfall

we write things to take thoughts off our minds and onto the pages that we live through
books are the storage spaces for our thoughts so we can make room for the new works.
libraries are a collective of these thoughts and through them we can view the human experience through another's eyes.

life fills like a glass on the wooden bar top
with distractions and detours to make the journey lasting
To find solace in glossed over eyes
until the glass runs over and
the thoughts that brought you there go away.

love is lasting and love is truth
in the light it is felt
in the dark it is devoid

when love is forced
it is superficial
when love is found
it is organic

when it is real
it is unlike anything else

take me to wherever you find happiness
i will surely return the favor by taking you to the
printing press to show you my friends -

the books that give ideas life, they give me the ability
to share what little experiences i have.

it’s not your words
i fell in love with,
it’s the fact that
you were the one
saying them.

i hope you find that our lives resemble
the tension between a wave and a shore

to love you is to chase the
a shadow of a love i'll never catch

oh how i wish
i could tell you again
to come to bed
i've been missing you

if love was a tangible object
it would be representative of
my fingers on your lips
with a taste of you in my mouth.

her ex
is my next to kin,
we’ve both lived
and died
seen floods and
the universe
all in one
person’s eyes

when the wind comes
so do the lights from far away lands

traveling the world to bless the eyes of our people

the waves bring words
the ink soaked seas bring a rugged
translation of far off screams.

save those who yell at the sea

to you,
you’re not forgotten.

did we choose to fall in love -
or was it by chance we fell with
no regard of the ground below

perhaps it was both
maybe we took each other's hand
stood next to the cliff
and waited for the wind

all i know is this:
i now love the wind and falling
in a perpetual motion alongside
you is the definition of living

the thing about love is that
it has no meaning before we
give it meaning

we decide the worth we give
love and the value it has

we decide to maintain our love
for ourselves and others

if we neglect this love
it dies within us

the passion of your touch after a time elapsed
is the equivalent of a rose bush blooming
in the spring earth

your petals fall to the floor assisted by
accelerated gravity

love and distance brings a new light for
the long nights.

in the age of fires we must not let the
oxygen fuel the mess
but let it give voices to those opposed
to the rage which was brought
by those unknowing the
impact of a pen.

if love is not the way we choose to live
then we will want nothing but
hate to thrive

for the unheard to be in a place of solace
is to place our future in a box.

the lights in my room love
morning company

when the floral scents follow the
scratches on a record player
we find notes only known by the
lillies and the roses

only known by slight touches and
long laughter

known by the pen
written by all

some days are better than others
for those in these positions of
hopeless downfalls fueled by
anxiety driven nerve endings.

a million and one needles
playing like piano keys on my
rose stained cheeks

closing the airways to my
well-being

to run is to hide from the truth that
is me

what controls you in the night
cannot conquer you in the day

love without fear
and tell them that
we will die when we are ready

she couldn’t feel the rain
even as it was pouring

you touched me and my skin went numb

but my heart has never felt so much at once

love in tangible
it's found within moments
captured in old photographs

love is found in a frame
where memories live

the days go slower when you
find no purpose in the motions

purpose is the reason words
exist on a page
every word has purpose and
knows its role in a sentence

i hope you find it

the thing in the place-
in the moment, that could
make your life look like
your imagination

i hope you find the innocence
in the fleeting moments

i hope you find it.

it’s okay to be in this moment
reading this and to think-
i wonder if this place is made for me

everything is naturally

uncertain

is this place made for me?

if you don’t put the
truths about your existence
into books - your thoughts
will be lost

we are not the same anymore
an honest assessment is that
we never will be again

if we get lucky enough
to find understanding tonight

we will be with the few who
have found both sides of such a feat

the nights feel like
the absence of air in my lungs

at an instance
moments turn into
memories without consent

to be remembered
but never replicated

as time moves
feelings fade into
background noise

at points it feels like
we live in the white noise

i have felt more alone
in a crowded room than
being in my apartment
surrounded by the essence of
nothingness

i envy the life of
someone who is okay
with comfort

let's be honest

our paths were blurry
to begin with

i don’t know how well we do
when we are alone

my words overlap and i have trouble
remembering the last thing i said to you

how did we get here again?

finding yourself is a journey one must make alone

when we love one another
it makes us realize
the importance of preserving
such an unknown beauty

our words are transformative
to the ways in which we
interpret the value of love

it is my dream to become
wealthy people that live
in the woods

filled with compassion

there was a moment
when i felt whole
knowing i would inevitably
be the villain
in someone else’s story

there is a strange comfort
in knowing that our paths will
never cross again

to uproot the things that are buried
seems to be the antagonist to
progression

in the world where we feel a need for
love - we must find it within
ourselves

spontaneity lacks the precision that
i crave to find understanding

yet the moments that lack understanding
feel like a home i have never known

to feel comfortable with the absence of understanding
is something i will never fully know

we need to find stability
in another to truly feel the love
that they can provide

without the knowingness of this
the unpredictability will eventually
erode the foundation that we once
set our life upon

the certainty of this comes from
once putting the essence of existence
on a platform thought to be concrete

i found the home of truth
in a place of misunderstanding

the reality is that one day
we will all be dead
in the ground or
somewhere else

if death found you today
would you be okay
with what you've done?

or would you wish
for one more chance

love at first sight
makes more sense
when you think that

love isn't an emotion
more so it is
naturally generated
when the world
deems it

if you come any closer
it will show you the impermanence
of me

once we find the reasoning
for being here - in this moment
it seems that the world will let us know

or maybe it is up to us to find the
moment and work it out for ourselves

i think that we will be okay
i’m not sure when, but i think we will be

we are meant to be
in harmony
such as the moon and the sea

if we never know why -
at least we know it
happened.

you and i
burned out
like lit matches
in the dark

darling,

i found that my innocence
was lost the moment i
allowed myself to lose it

never fearing that one day
i might miss the simplicity
it gave life

it seems apparent that
innocence is found through
the purity in moments
that lack the burdens
we have become accustomed to.

i would be doing both of us
a great injustice to not love you
with what little fragments i have left

it's at moments like this
that i begin to understand
the truth behind the words
that conceptualize forever

I hope you understand
that we may have never been soul mates -
But i appreciate the time we had together

it's the numbness in the liquid
that takes a toll on the body

to take away the feeling of pain
is to take away the sensations of happiness

in light of pain there is a momentary
lapse of judgment that convinces us
that tomorrow is bound to be the same

a day has opportunities we cannot
begin to dream about

a rebirth as the sun decides
to come around for another day

how lucky we should feel to
be in the midst of it all

it is the little things in life that
make us feel the array of colors

my days feel beige until a catalyst
finds its place in my mind
to change the hue

as dark as my palette might seem -
i feel as warm as the days sunset

some moments make us feel like
our worth is non-existent

just remember that light doesn’t
only emit from the sun

if i could describe you to someone -
it would be the experience of seeing
a picasso for the first time and feeling
the ridges of the paint

understanding that a one-of-a-kind piece
that holds such beauty is something that
cannot be replicated or reproduced

your essence is something that is immeasurable
and creates a longing unlike any other

we will find one another
in a moment that makes sense

when we will, for a second,
know why this life matters

i believe that these moments
are the reason we are here

moments are different than
lapses of time that feel
less than important
it's not that
a moment needs to hold an importance

it's that moments happen

and they matter

or not

i do know that you can feel a moment
in your soul

or

something

i have found moments are made
from divine intervention

the right chords in a song
whilst my eyes look at a certain
focal point

many times - it's your lips and smile

it would seem that
you're an important piece to these

moments

or at least were

one day we will all look back to
decide whether or not this life
that we will have lived was what
we wanted it to be

did we finally understand that this world
is ours to make what we want -
that what we have done matters

the difference between us
is that i think black
is a bright color

happiness and being fine
have never shared the
same space

i have lived lives that
were not mine whilst
loving another

we have fallen through
one another
like words
through
a hollow
promise

i believe that one day
we might find the world
to be ours for at least a moment

we come and go like the tides
that lead up to the shore
hoping to find a place to rest
for the remainder of our life

i’m not the person i used to be.

and for the first time ever -
i can say i’m okay with that.

i hope to find you
in the pauses of your breath
or in the midst of your
favorite notes

to find the reasoning
for the longing that
i feel inside my chest

we all find ourselves in this place
going through the human experience
without understanding why we are here

without knowing anything for certain
but knowing that we are all connected
by this world that we share
is something that no one can take from us

if we can accept that this jounrey is
meant to harbor love for one another
than we might find this world to make
a little more sense

www.ingramcontent.com/pod-product-compliance
Ingram Content Group UK Ltd.
Pitfield, Milton Keynes, MK11 3LW, UK
UKHW041643190726
13854UKWH00006B/2677